Keep It Simple...
Sweetheart

Dr. Fran Fisher

Griffin Publishing
8850 Auburn Folsom Road
Granite Bay, CA 95746

www.improveintimacy.com

Printed in the United States of America

For more information on Dr. Fran Fisher and her services, email:
drfran@improveintimacy.com
To order, visit www.improveintimacy.com

Fisher, Fran Dr.
Keep It Simple Sweetheart / Dr. Fran Fisher

1st Revision December 2004 2nd Revision April 2011
3rd Revision March 2012 4th Revision March 2014

ISBN-13: 978-0615612249
ISBN-10: 0615612245

1. Family & Relationships / Love & Romance 2. Family & Relationships /Education 3. Family & Relationships /Marriage 4. Family & Relationships /Reference 5. Family & Relationships /Aging 6. Self Help/Sexual Instruction 7. Self Help/Aging 8. Self Help/ General 9. Psychology/Human Sexuality 10. Psychology/Interpersonal Relations

Also, by Dr. Fisher:
In the Name of God, Why? Sexual Conversations with Former Catholic Nuns ISBN-13: 978-0615612225
ISBN-10: 0615612229
BISAC: Religion/Sexuality & Gender Studies

In respectful memory and grateful thanks for the inspirational quotes on the following pages from the late Frank Ostroff.

TABLE OF CONTENTS

Achieving Sexual and Spiritual Harmony
Respect without Judgment 4

Communication 8
   Asking for What We Want 10

Boredom in the Bedroom 12

Adapting to Life's Changes 15
   Pregnancy 15
   Menopause 18
   Illness 24
   General Aging 26

Female Arousal Difficulties 28
   Lack of Emotional Engagement 28
   Instructions & Advice for the Young Bride 32
   Stress and Depression 40
   Alcohol 40
   Physical Changes 41
   Fatigue 42

Erectile Difficulties 44
   Causes and Some Available Treatments 44
   Available Non-Surgical Treatments 46
   Surgical Treatments 48

Best Practices 49
   Safe Sex 50
   Oral Sex 54
   Play and Foreplay 57

Enhanced Intimacy and Extraordinary Sex
for Ordinary People 59
   It Begins with the Face in the Mirror 62
   The G Spot, Female Ejaculation and
   Multiple Orgasm.. 66
   Pubococcygeus Muscle Exercises for Women.............. 69
   Pubococcygeus Muscle Exercises for Men 71
   Sensate Focus Feature 73
   Hair Caress 75
   Foot Caress 78
   Face Caress 82
   Bathing Caress.. 86
   Body Caress.. 90
   Sexual Caress... 95

Summary.. 99

Resources 100
   Suggested Reading 100
   Helpful Books on Illness and Sexual Function 104
   Websites.. 105
   Publications Resources Supporting Prevention
      Activities & Survivor Healing...................................... 107
Education 108
Sexuality Video and Erotica Resources............................. 109

About the Author 110

Testimonials... 112

"Achieving intimacy requires the intentions to do so. Each partner must be open to give and receive whatever passes between the two.

This requires lowering or eliminating barriers and demands trust, which can't happen without honesty and the acceptance or each other's reality."

Jack William Small M.F.T.

KEEP IT SIMPLE SWEETHEART AND YOU MAY ACHIEVE SEXUAL AND SPIRITUAL HARMONY

- Do you ever feel afraid to tell your love partner a fantasy?

- Have you ever begun to share a sexual secret and stopped because of your partner's response? Even a subtle facial expression of disapproval can close down communication.

- Are you afraid your true inner self will be found out and you will be shamed?

- Have you ever felt your sexual needs are in conflict with your spiritual/religious beliefs?

I believe that to be fully in touch with their spiritual centers, human beings must honor their sexual natures. I have witnessed much unhappiness and personal damage caused by people denying that intimacy and sexual nurturing are fundamental to life.

Even those people who choose a life of celibacy are healthier when whey recognize and understand their sexual needs. Those who are thrust into a celibate life by the illness of a partner are also greatly helped by having their needs understood and validated.

Babies will not thrive unless they are touched. Adults may survive, but they too will not thrive unless they feel nurtured and loved. A respectful and loving touch contributes to that nurturing, and it is further enhanced when we feel sexually accepted and respected.

The cardinal rule of human sexuality is that no two people think or feel the same about it, and they do not have the same sexual knowledge. If you think you know what your neighbor or friend thinks or does sexually, you are deluding yourself. Further, if you do not communicate honestly and openly with your partner, opening your very essence to that person, you do not know what he or she feels about sex or understands about intimacy.

Remember, we will not open our hearts unless we feel safe to do so. Therefore, from the very beginning of a relationship, RESPECT WITHOUT JUDGMENT should be promoted as a way to intensify honest and open communication between partners. In my opinion, ignoring this intrinsic truth causes many difficulties in relationship and much marital discord.

"Carpenters, fashion wood; fletchers fashion arrows; the wise fashion themselves."

- Buddha

'Intimacy' is sharing the deep innermost essence of who you are with another person. It's showing your true self, warts and all.

Sexual Intimacy is a manifestation of emotional intimacy. You need the emotional intimacy to have the sexual intimacy."

-Masters & Johnson
Sex and Human Loving

COMMUNICATION
You talk, I listen! ... I talk, you listen!

This sounds simple. What often happens is that people speak into a vacuum, with neither partner truly being heard and understood. A simple two-minute exercise will test this theory:

- Set a clock and sit face-to-face.

- Choose who goes first. That person begins to talk. The other person simply listens, makes no verbal or nonverbal comment like facial expression.

- At the end of the two minutes, the listener repeats what he/she has heard. Begin with the words "I heard you say..." again with no defensive comments from the listener.

It is often quite a surprise to both partners that what is said is not what is heard. Sometimes we speak in terms that are just not clear. Repeating the dialogue leaves the door open for a better understanding.

- Now switch roles and repeat the exercise. Do this on a regular basis and you will become a more active listener.

Try this technique with your children and see the wonderful effects on your relationship with them too. Everyone appreciates being heard and understood.

Happily married couples aren't smarter, richer or more psychologically astute than others. But in their day-to-day lives, they have hit upon a dynamic that keeps their negative thoughts and feelings about each other (which all couples have) from overwhelming their positives ones. They have what I call an "emotionally intelligent marriage."

-John Gottman, Ph.D.

Asking for What We Want

Why is it easier for us to ask for a new car or a bedroom set than it is to ask for a foot caress? Why can we not ask to be cuddled without fearing it will lead to unwanted sexual activity? Where did we learn that asking for our emotional and sexual needs to be met is somehow wrong? Why do we allow bitterness and arguments to come before lovemaking? Where did we learn this kind of behavior?

Most people do not ask for their emotional and sexual needs to be met. Women more than men expect that miraculously their partner should understand and fulfill their needs. Too many men learn early in a relationship to expect little and to get it grudgingly.

Generally speaking, in our culture we meet new partners and try our best to please them. Life moves on. We get busy. We may have children, get even busier and think we know our partners so well that now we can rely on routine and memory to please them. We think it wrong and somehow degrading to ask for what we want sexually. Often couples do not think they need to grow and change their love-making techniques or add to their repertoire of skills. The Gold Standard of a hard penis and a juicy vagina is the traditional way to think about a good sex life. If this is the level you settle for, sex can become tedious and unexciting.

"When things don't work well in the living room they don't work well in the bedroom either."

Masters & Johnson

Boredom in the Bedroom

Don't be fooled. This can happen at quite an early stage. If you resist change throughout your relationship, boredom will slowly but surely corrode and erode that relationship. This process often goes unrecognized because of routine and busyness.

Statistics show that most marriages fail at regularly spaced periods:

- Seven to ten years when the babies arrive and job pressures are great.

- Thirteen plus years when the children and/or the pressure to succeed in business consume so much of the available time.

- Eighteen to twenty years when the children go away to college and you face a stranger across the table.

- Most surprising of all is the over fifty year old group who feel now or never and leave to find their last chance at happiness. Look around and notice the incidents of divorce in this age group seem to be increasing.

The tragedy is that subsequent marriages fail at a much more rapid rate because of additional pressures and complications of melded families. Even more curious is the fact that many times individuals maintain their friendships with their first partners. How would the first marriage have fared if the couple had addressed their lack of intimacy, sexual interaction and lack of sensual intensity early in their relationship?

"Some people change and forget to tell each other."

- Lillian Hellman

Adapting to Life's Changes

Pregnancy

Whether a woman is married or single the most dramatic disruption to any relationship comes in the form of the single biggest blessing-a baby. This transformation of relationship begins just after conception and continues for life. Today I hear too many couples express a belief that having a child should not disrupt their life in any way. They feel that day care and disposable diapers free them to live uninterrupted business and even social lives. But, everyone suffers when enough time isn't given to adapt. Stress builds and often couples disengage.

It takes time to adapt to all changes at this time; to go from a duo to a trio is a tremendous burden for some and requires a huge adjustment for all.

Issues come up constantly. Be open and prepared to talk about them honestly. Some of the topics and questions for women, men and couples to be aware of and open to discussing follow:

- How does it feel to have a baby inhabit and ultimately take over and alter your body?

- Does it scare you to have intercourse?

- Do you worry that it will hurt the baby?

15

- Do you worry if the baby will know and be traumatized?

- Have you wondered what oral sex will feel like during pregnancy and after the baby arrives?

- Will your husband/partner want to do it?

- Have you worried that you may not find your partner's vulva attractive after the birth?

- Is there the potential for conflict between lover/mother for the man?

- If a sexual relationship does not start again spontaneously following the birth, what should you do?

These are just a few common concerns. Your own personal questions are of vital importance to the success of your relationship and will need to be addressed and respected. Resources are available to allay your fears - just ask for them-seek them out.

If you cannot find answers to your questions, please consult an expert. Do it early rather than after your questions and confusions have become a major cause of concern.

"It is not only necessary to love, it is also necessary to say so…"

- French Saying

Menopause

Menopause is a huge trajectory change on the map of a woman's life; it is uncharted waters. Early onset of symptoms can begin in the thirties. Women, who go through early onset menopause following hysterectomy or chemotherapy, suffer all the same issues. Remember this is the first generation of menopausal women to be studied in long-term research that includes menopause.

Hormone Replacement Therapy (HRT) is a much-debated subject. Bio-identical hormone therapy is now the favored way to treat menopausal symptoms and there are some really good resources at the back of this book to help you learn more. Specialists are now available to help women with personal prescriptions to fit their symptoms. However, this form of treatment is not an option for all women, so doing your own research is crucial. The same advice holds true no matter what your favorite magazine tells you. BE YOUR OWN ADVOCATE.

To gain a thorough understanding of current knowledge on the subject, my recommendation is to read all you can from the extensive list of resources in the appendix. Then start a diary of symptoms and chart any that could be attributed to menopause. Once you have gathered a comprehensive list of symptoms for three months or more, take this list to your doctor and discuss options for treatment.

Make sure you understand what your doctor is telling you. Too often doctors use medical terms that can be confusing, and we are too embarrassed to ask for clarification. Remember also your doctor may have as little as five or ten minutes to spend with you. Make that time as useful as possible by being an informed patient. Your work will be appreciated, and your treatment plan will be more specific.

There are many over the counter remedies (OTC) dealing with everything from hot flashes to low libido. If you wish to keep a record of your symptoms for your doctor, do not use any OTC's during your fact finding months, as their effects may confuse your data.

If you are not collecting data and wish to try over-the-counter remedies, please be a label reader and a good researcher rather than simply believing expensive advertising. There is approximately a thirty percent positive placebo effect with all of these products. Use the product with the most female vitamins and minerals as well as the all-important ingredient, L-Arginine.

Some hints:

Vaginal dryness: Intercourse or any penetration should never hurt, no matter what your age. If it does hurt, stop until you can resolve the issue. As women age the tissue of the vagina changes, becomes thinner and more fragile. If you have difficulty talking to your partner about this sensitive subject, get the help of a sexuality counselor to help you.

A helpful hint for vaginal dryness during intercourse at any age is for women to give themselves time to lubricate naturally. This usually means allowing time for foreplay to achieve at least one orgasm before penetration. This can be achieved with oral stimulation, manually or with a vibrator. Going straight to intercourse without any prior stimulation does not give a women time to emotionally engage and the result can be painful. Approximately seventy-five percent of women require clitoral stimulation in order to become aroused. That means that approximately twenty-five percent of women enjoy vaginal orgasm without clitoral stimulation. So relax and enjoy your clitoris. This little tip may solve the problem in many cases.

For persistent complaints of vaginal dryness, which can impact a woman in a variety of non-sexual ways, I recommend the use of vaginal lubricants. There are two kinds of lubricants, moisturizers and sealants. Moisturizers penetrate the tissue, a regular program of morning and evening massage of the entrance to the vagina & internally with a gentle finger followed by gently massaging the external genitals as well will help heal the fragile tissues. Sealants stay on the surface and stay slippery helping to protect delicate skin from the effects of friction. Some examples of moisturizers are Aloe Cadabra, Good Clean Love, Slippery Stuff & Coconut Oil. Examples of moisturizers with sealant would be Liquid Silk, Sliquid Organic Silk, KY Intrigue and Kama Sutra Love Liquid. When any penetration is involved, either with intercourse or sex toys, lube should be applied to both partner and toy liberally.

Avoid products with Glycerin, warming, cooling or stimulating properties, mineral oil or vegetable oil (OK for moisturizing but not for penetration).

For women who experience vaginal dryness so severely that they bleed even when doing such things as riding a bicycle, I strongly suggest they speak with their oncologists, their hormone specialists and their gynecologists to perhaps find a combination of treatments that may help relieve these disabling symptoms. Don't be afraid to talk to your doctors about Bio Identical Hormone replacement therapy for vaginal rehabilitation following chemotherapy. This is a quality of life issue and there are compounding pharmaceuticals designed to assist with this problem. Don't be afraid to ask.

In the meantime, I recommend the couple consult with a sex sensitive and supportive counselor to get helpful ideas about ways to adapt their sexual practice until this problem can be resolved. Additionally couples very often need help to open communication about their feelings surrounding the diagnosis, surgery, treatments and prognosis involved when a life threatening disease is diagnosed.

Loss of libido: Do not be afraid to mention this condition to your doctor. Having your hormones checked will give you a base line to measure exactly where your levels are.

There is a great deal of debate at present concerning testosterone use for women. Because this issue is in the forefront of research and is still a subject of much controversy amongst the experts, I encourage every woman who is undergoing hormone testing to insist on having her testosterone levels checked also. Take this information to a hormone expert for analysis.

Every woman is unique; there is no "one size fits all" cure for symptoms. It is good news today to see the medical profession finally waking up to this truth.

Remember, if you don't use it you lose it! Research by Masters and Johnson demonstrated that women who had regular intercourse maintained vaginal lubrication long after menopause.

"THE HEALING
POWER OF
INTIMACY —

I am not aware of any other
factor in medicine - not diet, not
smoking, not stress, not genetics,
not drugs, not surgery, that has a
greater impact on the quality of
our life, incidence of illness and
premature death from all causes."

-Dean Ornich, M.D.

Illness

None of us is ever prepared for the moment when illness comes into our lives. In a moment it impacts us and forever changes the personal relationships in our lives. Ill health also demands changes in the techniques of lovemaking that have become so comfortable. Change is the most difficult thing to cope with; human beings like routine, stability and their love life to be "safe, the way it always was." Sometimes couples become celibate rather than embrace the challenge of learning a new way of demonstrating their love on a physical level. Or, they continue to do things the way they always have and suffer pain and discomfort rather than embrace something new.

Help is available to assist even the most physically impair individual to learn adaptive sexual skills. However, one must ask for it and be prepared to change. More often than not, doctors are skilled at treating the physical condition, but they totally ignore the sexual ramifications that come along with a diagnosis. Until doctors become more comfortable discussing intimacy and sexuality, the patient or relative is going to have to be proactive in seeking help. Educational resources are included in the appendix.

Sometimes it may be necessary to seek expert help when sexuality and illness become overwhelming. Having a safe place to express these issues can often relieve a lot of pain. A trouble shared is a trouble halved.

"The love we have in our youth is superficial compared to the love that an older man has for his older wife."

-Will Durant

General Aging

Much of the recent research dispels the myth that as we get older we stop being sexual. The images of dirty old men or frisky old ladies are thankfully giving way to a more respectful recognition of the fact that, no matter how old we are, we desire and thrive on loving touch and can enjoy an active sex life until the end of our days.

How we "do" sex must necessarily alter with the challenges life brings us. However, the fact that older people are having sex and having great sex is indisputable.

At a recent seminar, a discussion about the beauty of mature love elicited a response from a gentleman in his seventies who was there with his wife. He said, "When I look into the eyes of my wife of forty years, I see directly into her soul, experiencing only the beauty and love of our life together."

Another comment from a participant was "when I look into her eyes, I see her as I did when we first met, over forty years ago."

"The omnipresent process of sex, as it is woven into the whole texture of a man's or woman's body, is the pattern of all the process of our life."

-Havelock Ellis

Female Arousal Difficulties

Lack of Emotional Engagement

Difficulty with sexual arousal is a very common problem and has received quite a lot of press recently. Reports indicate that forty-three percent of women in the United States have some level of sexual dysfunction. It is not dysfunctional to lack desire for sex that is coercive, painful, disrespectful, boring or lacking emotional connectedness. It may be that, at least for some of those forty million women, a sense of their own personal integrity and responsibility is the reason for their lack of sexual desire, and this is a very healthy response.

She must feel validated in her assessment of the quality of lovemaking for a woman to take an honest approach to improving her personal experience. She must also be given the power to realize that she can take the steps necessary to change her love life, have the relationship she wants, and have it with the partner she already has.

As mentioned, the menopausal woman often experiences low-to-no libido, as does the pregnant or new mother. Educating women of all ages to discover their own bodies and their potential for self-pleasure is very freeing. Full self-knowledge must come before they launch into ill-considered partnered sex in order to discover the "forbidden pleasures" or rely on partners to always know how to pleasure them. If women were

28

more secure and comfortable in their self-exploration and confident with experimenting in self-pleasuring, they would become more responsible for their own orgasms. This practice would give them personal knowledge, insights and control over their own bodies and encourage them to explore their pleasure zones. It is very empowering to be able to share this knowledge when the time comes to choose partners rather than depending on others for sexual satisfaction. The burden on sexual partners is extreme when women are totally ignorant of their own bodies. In this situation, the partner has to be responsible for both their own sexual fulfillment as well as their partners. Additionally, younger women would, in my opinion, be less likely to rush into ill-considered sexual activity if they were allowed to know their own bodies and honor their own needs. Historically when women were considered asexual (non-sexual), one could understand this type of fear around female sexuality. It is extraordinary to realize how many women (and men) still maintain this belief. I see it as a win-win for couples when both have the ability and responsibly to satisfy themselves on their own timetables, joining in lovemaking only when it is mutually desired not as a duty.

It has been estimated that ten percent to fifteen percent of women have not experienced an orgasm or, for various reasons do not recognize their own orgasms. No matter the age of a woman in this situation, you are never too old to address this. I encourage them to seek help from a sex therapist or counselor. There is help and you personally deserve a full and healthy sexual experience; it is your birthright. You have a clitoris for no other reason than pleasure; it's yours, feel free to release yourself from the misery today.

As unbelievable as it may seem in the twenty-first century, masturbation is still a taboo subject in many homes and more broadly, in our entire culture. Some people may remember the Surgeon General of the United States, Jocelyn Elders, was fired by Bill Clinton's administration because she discussed masturbation in positive terms at an international conference. I will refrain from comment on this hypocrisy as it serves little purpose here.

I simply propose that maintaining a healthy practice of self-pleasuring enhances, and in no way detracts from healthy sexuality and a happy couple's lovemaking. I understand that for many religious couples this is not an acceptable statement. At the same time I witness so much pressure and unwanted sexual activity leading to discontent that I must reiterate the need for open dialogue on this subject.

"Before the 1960's people who wrote books on sex stated with an almost religious fervor that playing with yourself (masturbation) was a very bad thing to do Today people who write books on sex speak with the same kind of religious fervor, only now they say that playing with yourself is a very good thing to do."

-Guide to Getting it On!

It is helpful to understand the source for many of our restrictions on sexual behavior in order to overcome them. Read through the following sermon given to the young bride on her wedding day, take a highlighter pen and notice how many of the instructions given in 1894 still resonate with you today. If five generations of women were to sit in a room and discuss sexuality, you could understand that the messages from the elders would carry many of the messages from this sermon.

**Instructions and
Advice for the
Young Bride On
the
Conduct and Procedures of the
Intimate and Personal
Relationships of the Marriage
State**

For the
Greater Spiritual Sanctity of this
Blessed Sacrament and the Glory of God

By Ruth Smythers

Beloved wife of the Reverend L.D. Smythers
Pastor of the Arcadian Methodist Church of the
Eastern Regional Conference

Published in the year of Our Lord 1894
Spiritual Guidance Press
New York

Instruction and Advice for the Young Bride

"To the sensitive young woman who has had the benefits of proper upbringing, the wedding day is, ironically, both the happiest and the most terrifying day of her life. On the positive side, there is the wedding itself, in which the bride is the central attraction in a beautiful and inspiring ceremony symbolizing her triumph in securing a male to provide for all her needs for the rest of her natural life. On the negative side there is the wedding night, during which the bride must pay the piper, so to speak, by facing for the first time the terrible experience of sex.

At this point, dear reader let me concede one shocking truth. Some young women actually anticipate the wedding night ordeal with curiosity and pleasure! Beware such an attitude! A selfish and sensual husband can easily take advantage of such a bride. One cardinal rule of marriage should never be forgotten: GIVE LITLE, GIVE SELDOM AND ABOVE ALL, and GIVE GRUDGINGLY. Otherwise, what could have been a proper marriage could become an orgy of sensual lust.

On the other hand, the bride's terror need not be extreme. While sex is at best revolting and at worse rather painful, it has to be endured, and has been by women since the beginning of time, and is compensated for by the monogamous home and by the children produced through it.

It is useless, in most cases, for the bride to prevail upon the groom to forgo the sexual initiation. While the ideal husband would be one who would approach his bride only at her request and only for the purpose of begetting offspring, such nobility and unselfishness cannot be expected from the average man.

Most men, if not denied, would demand sex almost every day. The wise bride will permit a maximum of two brief sexual experiences weekly during the first months of marriage. As time goes by she should make every effort to reduce this frequency.

Feigned illness, sleepiness, and headaches are among the wife's best friends in this matter. Arguments, nagging, scolding and bickering also prove very effective, if used in the late evening about an hour before the husband would normally commence his seduction.

Clever wives are ever on the alert for new and better methods of denying and discouraging the amorous overtures of the husband. A good wife should expect to have reduced sexual contacts to once a week by the end of the first year of marriage and to once a month by the end of the fifth.

By their tenth anniversary many wives have managed to complete their child bearing and have achieved the ultimate goal of terminating all sexual contacts with the husband. By this time she can depend upon his love for the children and social pressures to hold the husband in the home.

Just as she should ever be alert to keep the quality of sex as low as possible, the wise bride will pay equal to limiting the kind and degree of sexual contacts. Most men are by nature rather perverted, and if given half a chance, would engage in quite a variety of the most revolting practices. These practices include, among others, performing the normal sex act in abnormal positions, mouthing the female body, and offering their own vile bodies to be mouthed in turn.

Nudity, talking about sex, reading stories about sex, viewing photographs and drawing depicting or suggesting sex are other obnoxious habits the male is likely to acquire if permitted.

A wise bride will make it her goal never to allow her husband to see her unclothed body. And never allow him to display his unclothed body to her. Sex, when it cannot be prevented, should be practiced only in total darkness. Many women have found it useful to have thick cotton nightgowns for themselves and pajamas for their husbands. These should be donned in separate rooms. They need not be removed during the sex act. Thus a minimum of flesh is exposed.

Once the bride has donned her gown and turned off all the lights she should lie down quietly across the bed and await her groom. When he comes groping into the room she should make no sound to guide him in her direction, lest he take this as a sign of encouragement. She should let him grope in the dark. There is always the hope that he will stumble and incur some slight injury, which she can use as an excuse to deny him sexual access.

When he finds her, the wife should lie as still as possible. Bodily motion on her part could be interpreted as sexual excitement by the optimistic husband.

If he attempts to kiss her on the lips she should turn her head slightly so that he falls harmlessly on her cheek instead. If he attempts to kiss her she should make a fist. If he lifts her gown and attempts to kiss her anywhere else she should quickly pull the gown back in place, spring from the bed, and announce that nature calls her to the toilet. This will generally dampen his desire to kiss in forbidden territory.

If the husband attempts to seduce her with lascivious talk, the wise wife will suddenly remember some trivial nonsexual question to ask him. Once he answers she should keep the conversation going, no matter how frivolous it may seem at the time. Eventually the husband will learn that if he insists on having sexual contact he must get on with it without amorous embellishment. The wise wife will allow him to pull the gown up no further than the waist, and only permit him to open the front of his pajamas to thus make connection.

She will be absolutely silent or babble about her housework while he is huffing and puffing away. Above all, she will lie perfectly still and never under any circumstances grunt or groan while the act is in progress.

As soon as the husband has completed the act, the wise wife will start nagging him about various minor tasks she wishes him to perform on the morrow. Many men obtain a major portion of their sexual satisfaction from the peaceful exhaustion immediately after the act is over. Thus the wife must insure that there is no peace in this period for him to enjoy. Otherwise, he might be encouraged to try for more.

One heartening factor for which the wife can be grateful is the fact that the husband's home, church, and social environment have been working together all through his life to instill in him a deep sense of guilt in regards to his sexual feeling, so that he comes to the marriage couch apologetically and filled with shame, already half cowed and subdued. The wife seizes upon this advantage and relentlessly pursues her goal first to limit, later to annihilate completely her husband's desire for sexual expression."

Sadly, couples still experience many of the myths expressed in this piece with disastrous results on their relationship and level of intimacy.

It is heartening that in 2001 the former Surgeon General Dr. David Satcher published his "Surgeon General's Call To Action To Promote Health and Responsibility." He very clearly advocated for sexuality education to be scientifically based on facts, not on fiction, fear, and fabrication. I would encourage you to get a copy of this paper; it is well written and informative. Later I will refer to some of Satcher's findings in my Sexually Transmitted Disease Chapter.

When a couple is troubled by low to no libido, whether it be the woman or the man experiencing the issue, honest acknowledgment of difficulties and taking time out to do some active listening is the beginning of the process of healing. Getting help from a sex-positive counselor is also recommended; otherwise couples can spend months in therapy without ever touching on the core issues of sexual frustration and unhappiness with the level of intimacy.

"The first duty of Love

is to listen."

-Paul Tillich

Stress and Depression

If relationships slip into isolation and antagonism, we often experience depression. Sometimes its onset may cause sexual dysfunction. The one fact here is that depression and its treatment, i.e., most antidepressants, impact sexual function.

Because some anti-depressants have less effect on sexual function than others, always ask your doctor or pharmacist for the sexual side effects of any medication before you take it.

Even though it is common knowledge that sexual release is a great stress reducer, too often it is the last thing we think of to create a "feel good" moment. We turn to medication, smoking and...

Alcohol

One or two drinks may reduce sexual inhibition, but multiple drinks can have a depressive effect. As we age, alcohol has an even stronger negative effect on sexual function.

When relationships turn sour, we sometimes rely on drinking to "put us in the mood." This is like having sex while we are unconscious. It's not only in rocky relationships where this kind of alcohol induced sexual action happens. You only have to go to a nightclub or student dance to see the sexual acting out of alcohol and drug-induced loss of inhibition.

Although the emphasis in our schools' sex education is on abstinence until marriage, we often fail to stress the vulnerability to sexual acting out when under the influence of alcohol. Most initial sex acts in school or college age people take place after the consumption of alcohol or the use of illicit drugs. Effective sex education of our youth requires more inclusive recognition of the need for factual and frank discussion of their emotional health and quality of life issues.

Physical Changes

In our Madison Avenue society, probably the biggest negative effects on a woman's sexual desire and function are the physical changes that occur naturally during pregnancy and the general aging process.

As you read earlier in another section of this book, the beauty of a loved one is unchanged in the eyes of the beholder no matter how old that person is. Obesity is now becoming a medical crisis in this country. I wonder if we fed our intimate needs to the degree we feed our physical body, we could go a long way to reducing the cravings to eat with no regard as to the damage it does to our sex lives.

Maintaining a healthy body and loving oneself first, then sharing that love wholeheartedly is the best recipe for life long respect and intimacy. Some of the sexiest women and men in the world are over fifty.

Fatigue

Americans are among the hardest-working people on the planet. It is recognized around the world that Americans take fewer vacations, work longer hours, live harder and faster. Often, when relationships are strained, partners avoid the resulting pressure by increasing the workload and decreasing the time at home. Yet, allowing time and energy for intimacy and lovemaking is essential to the health and well-being of a relationship. If there are children, one must realize that family happiness depends on the continuity of parental love. Couples should be encouraged to allow time in their busy schedules to concentrate on themselves. I heartily endorse parents meeting the needs of their children; however, sometimes they must shift their priorities back to themselves. After all, divorce is the quintessential destruction of family values.

"Having dealt with the theoretical aspect of the art of loving, we are now confronted with a much more difficult problem, that of "the practice of the art of loving." Can anything be learned about the practice of an art, except by practicing it?"

-Erick Fromm, Ph.D.

Erectile Difficulties

Causes and Some Available Treatments

One of the "scariest" things to happen to a man is when he first realizes he has erectile difficulties. Even a one-time event in a younger man can be so traumatic that it begins a cycle which causes stress and eventually results in a self-fulfilling prophecy and it starts to be a chronic problem.

An often-told story comes out of the Vietnam War when a soldier woke up from serious lower body injuries. The soldier's first words were said to be "Thank God, I'm alive" and the second words were, after looking down at their penis, "Oh God, will it still work." Even as we acknowledge the tremendous pressure on a man to "perform" we must add a suggestion to try and grow and expand beyond the boundaries of penis vagina as the only way to "do" sex.

Historically, people didn't talk about these problems. This must have taken a terrible toll on their relationships. It is fair to say that until the advent of Viagra, we had no idea of the vast numbers of men who were suffering in silence. It is estimated that, in America alone, thirty million men suffer some level of erectile difficulty. This number covers a wide age span. It is a myth that only older men have erectile dysfunction.

Bob Dole gave permission for men to say, "Well if he can talk on TV about his problem, maybe I can go to my doctor and ask for help too."

Anything that impacts the circulatory system impacts the erectile tissue of the penis:

- Smoking

- Excessive alcohol intake

- Diabetes

- High blood pressure and medications to control it.

- Coronary artery disease and heart surgeries and their associated medications.

- Anxiety is one of the biggest problems impacting sexual function generally. Post cardiac event patients and their partners experience a new level of fear when they think they may die from the exertion of sex. Rehabilitation should include a thorough human sexuality component in order to inform and reassure the patient and partner of the safe practices following the diagnosis of heart disease.

- Pelvic trauma of any kind can impact erections.

- Medications, both over the counter and prescription, are known to affect many areas of sexual function from the desire phase to inhibiting orgasms even when highly aroused. Check with your pharmacist if you are taking any medication and notice an unusual effect on your sex drive or function.

- Stress and depression have a profound effect on all areas of human function. A man's ability to become aroused and have healthy erections is often stalled by complex emotional issues.

Available Non-Surgical Treatments

- External vacuum therapy or pump, least invasive

- Over the counter supplements Yohimbine and Aveena Sativa (extract of common oats), Arginmaxx are sexual aides

- Prescription Medications: Because dosage strength varies, your doctor will establish your personal needs at the time of your consultation.

Before using any of the following medications it is advised that a couple meet with a sex-positive counselor to transition smoothly back into intercourse if it has been some time since a full sex life has been enjoyed. These medications have been a miracle for many men and some have required help in rekindling their relationship for complete success.

- Viagra (Sildenafil Citrate). An oral medication prescribed by your doctor, Viagra can be taken one hour before sexual activity and can be repeated daily. Latest research shows that the onset of effectiveness began as early as fifteen minutes.

- Levitra (Vardenifil HCl)
  An oral prescription treatment of erectile dysfunction. Works very similarly to Viagra. It is recommended that this medication be taken approximately one hour before sexual activity and the dosage prescribed by your doctor can be repeated daily.

- Cialis (Tadalafil) differs from the two previous medications in that it is shown to effect erectile function up to thirty-six hours following dosing. Therefore to assess your needs safely, use caution when first taking this medication. Speak to your doctor if you suffer from any medical condition, which would prohibit you having medication in your system for this length of time.

Speak to your doctor about any concerns or questions you may have about all the treatments available.

- Muse (Alprostadil) Urethral suppository:
  The partner needs to use a condom since the drug passes upon ejaculation and may cause headaches)

- Self-injection therapy (caverject)

With all of these treatments for erectile dysfunction, an erection lasting more than four hours is considered a medical emergency and immediate treatment should be sought at the Emergency Department.

Surgical Treatments

- Penile prosthetic implants

- Semi-rigid

- Self-contained inflatable

- Multi-component inflatable

A urologist will diagnose and prescribe the best treatment. If necessary the patient can get advice about introducing these new methods into a loving relationship from a sex-positive counselor. Once again, consider this resource if you feel anxiety about using these devices and treatments.

Best Practices

It is an incontrovertible fact that exercise and diet should be primary concerns of all health conscious people. The level at which we exercise is of course governed by our overall health. Always check with your physician before starting an exercise program but start one today! Add yoga to your work out. In our fast paced lives this activity helps us focus, slow down, and, as we age, keep our joints and muscles loose and limber — an added bonus to a Kama Sutra pose!

Don't forget that sexual intercourse is considered a great way to exercise. You can become aerobic and release endorphins in the brain, both of which lead to stress relief and a feeling of good health. The added benefit not found at the gym is that at the end of a good work out in bed you get to cuddle with your lover.

Diet and exercise afford excellent opportunities for a couple to share a common activity. Have you ever thought of adding food to your sex play? Let your imagination run wild and have fun.

For some great tips, visit my website:
www.improveintimacy.com

Safe Sex

I think this is the first generation where people over the age of forty need to be educated about safe sex practices. Condoms were virtually never the concern of a woman, nor were they common in girl/boy friend or gay relationships in the past.

Prior to the 1960's, middle-aged people bought into the idea that they were too old for THAT. Additionally, divorce in later life was very rare. The sexual revolution gave young people a false sense of complacency because of the easy availability of antibiotics. Even the dreaded killer Syphilis had been tamed. Primarily because of the advent of the AIDS epidemic, many proffer the belief that disease and sex are synonymous and at the same time the 60's sex revolutionaries are still not comfortable using condoms. It is important however, to remember that condoms do not protect against all sexually transmitted diseases (STDs). Chlamydia, genital warts (papilloma virus), gonorrhea and genital herpes are among the infections that can be passed on by skin contact from an infected person.

My first warning is to be aware that all unprotected sex has the potential to expose an unsuspecting person to STIs. It's a crapshoot whether that infection is one of the lists of STI's including HIV. Therefore, the message is to take care, be responsible for yourself.

Viral Hepatitis is of great concern because the carrier is often asymptomatic (that means they may show no signs of illness in the early stages which may last for years). The numbers of people infected with sexually transmitted hepatitis is staggering, and with flu like symptoms being the only indicator of infection, people go undiagnosed for years until they begin to exhibit serious signs of illness.

Dr. David Satcher's 'Call To Action' states, "Five of the ten most commonly reported infectious diseases in the U.S. are STDs; and in 1995, STDs accounted for eighty percent of cases reported among those ten. Nevertheless, public awareness regarding STDs is not widespread, nor is their disproportionate impact on women, adolescents, and racial and ethnic minorities well known." As informed people we need to educate ourselves with all the latest information available from the CDC website (see appendix). So armed you must educate your children, your sex partner, your co-workers, anyone having sex who could possibly be in jeopardy needs to be made aware of the potential for infection and the means by which you can protect yourself. Simply having sex with the light on so that you can actually check out your partner would be a good start. Not having sex until you can both be checked out by your doctor and being in the room for the results is even better. BUT, given the fact that this may not always be practical at least be in charge of your own health and well-being by asking questions about your potential partner's sexual health history that person is usually so surprised by the question that you MAY just get the truth.

That message is, of course, relevant to all ages of the sexually active population. But I am particularly addressing those who are entering into sexual relationships after a long period out of the dating scene. Things have changed. You really need to know how to use a condom!

I was giving a talk not long ago to a group of older adults and demonstrated the use of a condom over my head! After the talk a woman in her late forties came up to me and asked if I could give her a condom so that she could practice with it. She was divorced, dating, and had never used a condom in her life. She told me it had never occurred to her that she might be at risk. Tragically, one of the fastest growing groups of HIV infected people is "over sixties." The advent of Viagra has encouraged more sexual activity among the retired population, and they often don't use any protection.

Finally if you enjoy anal sex the use of a condom is highly advised. And always remember anything that goes into an anus must be attached to a human being or have a large flange on it. If a dildo or any foreign body goes up into the rectum, it can often be very difficult to remove and requires an embarrassing trip to the emergency room and may even involve dangerous surgery to remove it. Keep in mind also that when having anal/vaginal penetration, it's safe to go from vagina to anus but NEVER from anus to vagina. The bacteria in the bowel can cause severe infections. ALWAYS use a condom for anal play.

"The life which
is unexamined is
not worth
living."

-Socrates / Plato

Oral Sex...

Is it sex or isn't it???

Former President Clinton opened up an interesting dialogue in America that had previously not been known in the general public. The discussion was based on whether oral sex was indeed sex at all?

In my opinion, the degree of intimacy required to perform this type of lovemaking would logically require a deep knowledge and respect for the partner. This, however, does not appear to be the cultural norm at this time. It seems that many people consider only penetration to be actual sex. This is an interesting throw back to the era in history about one hundred years ago, when doctors could masturbate their female patients to orgasm in order to cure their "Hysteria," (this was never seen as sexual because women were considered asexual and were not being penetrated). However, when the speculum was invented there was a huge outcry because penetration was involved.

In another comparison of mental gymnastics, there are cultures where men and women engage in anal sex prior to marriage and feel this preserves the woman's right to call herself a virgin. The way we think about sexuality is fascinating and is all fodder for great debate.

When it comes to Safe Sex, and if you don't your partner's full sexual medical history, always use a condom for penetration as well as for oral sex on a man (they make nice tasting ones now). You can use cling film over a woman's genitals if you don't have a dental dam. Look for any skin blemishes around the genitals before making any contact...that means have the light on.

Hygiene is an extremely important prelude to enjoying oral sex. Always take a shower or bath before engaging in oral pleasure. Bathing together gives you the opportunity to wash your lover making sure you feel confident in their cleanliness as well as having time to check for skin blemishes and sores.

You can keep a thermos with warm, moist towels by the bedside so that you can freshen up at any time without disturbing the moment.

Some women do not like the taste or smell of their own genitals; this could actually be the topic of another book, so partners should remember to ask this before moving from kissing the genitals to kissing their partner on the mouth. Please refer to Kenneth Ray Stubbs', *A Fun Guide To Oral Sex* for some good ideas, do's and don'ts about the practice.

"Awake, in dream, I come
upon you there, fire in the
vein to fill my most great need
and you deny me nothing"

We Are All Secret Loves

-Lawrence Lipton

Play and Foreplay

Foreplay can take hours. We are conditioned to think that the reason for foreplay is to get the juices flowing, allowing easier entry of the penis. I want to dispel this myth and stress that the reason for foreplay is to play, to allow a couple lots of time to enjoy the exquisite pleasure of each other's bodies and explore how to be sensual as well as sexual.

As previously discussed, many young women complain of dryness and pain during intercourse. When they have at least one orgasm before penetration, they often find they are lubricating much more. If a woman isn't really turned on, she will not lubricate. She needs time to connect and become emotionally engaged.

"Laughter is the shortest distance between two people."

- Victor Borg

Enhanced Intimacy and Extraordinary Sex for Ordinary People

We live in a pleasure phobic society, a touch starved culture. This was not always the case. A glance into history illustrates the beauty and abundance of sensual, sexual art. Any conceivable sexual position or eroticism has been tried, documented, filmed, or written about. It is hard to believe the Kama Sutra is nothing more than a collection of pictures from Hindu Temples still standing today in Kajaroho, India! Imagine a day when such honor could be given to sexual expression!

After the sexual excesses of the 1960's, we are in the pendulum swing of prohibition on sexual, sensual pleasure. The end result for many is a complete loss of intimacy in relationships and transference of our emotional needs to our children, our jobs and our churches. We fill up our lives with over scheduling, taking away from the simplicity of childhood and emotionally disengaging from our partners. It is time to bring a little common sense to the paranoia. Those attending my workshops do so in order to learn, to broaden their horizons, or to gain information that will help them break out of the lonely, isolated, unfulfilling practices in which they find them- selves trapped.

Remember that every sexual act should be between consenting adults. It is never okay to pressure or manipulate in order to get what we want sexually; that equals abuse in my opinion. Children should never be exposed to adult sexuality. Teaching children from an early age to respect their parents' privacy is essential to healthy development in their own lives ahead as well as giving parents time and privacy to maintain a loving relationship. Make it a practice to have a date night at least once a month. Telling children Mom and Dad's closed bedroom door means the parents must not be disturbed, establishes respectful boundaries. Hugging and kissing in front of the children, however, demonstrates love and affection and is appropriate behavior. Also parents can give one another foot, head, and back caresses while watching TV and thereby illustrate loving touch to their children in a non-sexual way. Children love to have their backs tickled and stroked; why not Mom and Dad? Given those preliminary basic rules, everything else between lovers is negotiable. How do we change our lives and allow ordinary people to experience extraordinary sex?

"There is no norm in sex. Norm is the name of a guy in Brooklyn."

-Alex Comfort, Ph.D.

It Begins With the Face in the Mirror

See your own sexuality.
See it, Own it, Celebrate it!!

Don't be discouraged, this process may take some time and you may need professional help to dispel the messages of the past. Nevertheless, keep working toward that goal of mental freedom.

Think back to moments in your life when sex and sensual pleasure were more important than food or sleep (even the most modest of us have such memories). Try to rekindle that magic. Fantasies are the stuff of dreams and kindling for the fire of passion. It is not disloyal to remember a former lover or experience. This is fantasy, not reality, and you do not have to share your thoughts aloud. Develop a rich fantasy life. It keeps your brain alive.

What you must share and speak about are your needs and desires. Ask for what you want 100 percent of the time. Be willing to hear NO, but then negotiate a win, win. That means learn to give as much pleasure as you wish for yourself and communicate. Maybe you would enjoy a little outside assistance. Be open to talking about some of your sexual fantasies that may be sparked by reading erotic stories or watching erotic movies. The selection of videos has mushroomed over the past years with some very tasteful work directed and produced by women. Sex educational videos can also be very useful. Be open to the material available, and be honest about your own response.

Here are some hints for you:

- Putting the emphasis on PLAY rather than on SEX brings sensuality more into FOREPLAY; therefore, massage oils and stroking are important elements to add in the mix. Don't forget non-sexual foot, hand, face and head caresses. Read about Sensate Focus later in this book and add these exercises to your intimate times.

- Erotic toys will add a great deal of fun and pleasure to sex play as well as being highly recommended for some sexual dysfunctions.

- When you think about sexual play, think about dressing up rather than undressing. Remember when you were a child and dressing up was such fun?

- Use your imagination. Take sex out of the bedroom. In our busy lives, we often see the bed and want nothing more than to snuggle down and sleep. Even worse, many people bring their laptops to bed and then watch the news as their pre-sleep entertainment!

- If the bedroom is the only available private space, then add a special bedspread to signify Play Time, and, if necessary make sure to schedule time (a play date) if you have to.

- Some clients have reported that stopping any late night news viewing in the bedroom and establishing the habit of allotting fifteen minutes a night for each to ask for whatever she/he needs helps both to settle down to sleep peacefully in a loving space. There can be no sexual agenda attached to this fifteen minutes; such pressure is the kiss of death to this practice.

Examples of my suggestions are a back massage, cuddling, spooning (that means to lie in each other's arms nestled like two spoons), lying close while stroking each other or taking turns to be totally spoiled with bodily attention, talking about something warm and loving (not jobs for tomorrow or stresses of the day). Bathing together, reading a chapter from an erotic story or book of fantasies are other suggestions. Quite often these fifteen minutes continue much longer; however, people look forward to this precious shared time with no pressure to perform after their busy frantic day. It helps build trust between partners and allows women, particularly, to relax and be close and loving because the no agenda rule gives permission for them to ask for what they need without fear of their request being misinterpreted. Sexual life when it is planned or happens spontaneously is very much improved by time spent on improving intimacy.

- Add music and candles to your bedroom or play area; talk erotically to each other; tell stories.

- Don't be afraid of the Internet. It is a tremendous source of information on health issues as well as on sexual material. If you notice an increase in unsolicited mail, simply delete it without opening.

- Do you like to be spanked? Are you curious about Sadomasochism (S&M) or Bondage & Discipline (B&D)? Leather goods and S&M paraphernalia are available in stores or online if this is your fantasy.

These two particular fetishes must be very thoroughly explored together. It is imperative that both partners are in full agreement and that no coercion is involved. There are clubs and groups where you can get more information as well as many professional articles and academic papers written on the subject. The Internet is the best place to get all the answers you need.

The G Spot, female ejaculation and multiple ORGASMS

In the early 1980's, John Perry and Beverly Whipple published studies in which they identified an area of increased vaginal sensitivity on the front wall over a spongy area of the urethra (a short tube connecting the bladder to the urethral opening, located just above the vaginal opening).

Ninety percent of the subjects reported an area on the front wall of the vagina just inside the introitus (from the Latin for "entrance"), which was highly sensitive. In further studies, a nurse or doctor examined more than four hundred female volunteers all of whom reported similar findings. As a mark of respect for the pioneering work of the German obstetrician Ernst Grafenberg, Perry and Whipple named the G spot after him.

Experimenting to find your G spot is a fun experience for single play and couple's. Specially shaped sexual aides are available to help you locate the right area. Again, read all you can about these fun, undiscovered erogenous zones and be prepared to experiment.

Female Ejaculation: In my practice I have met women who explain that they reach high levels of excitement, feel as if they are going to climax, but then hold back and don't ever experience sexual release. They often believe that they urinate upon orgasm and are so embarrassed they refuse to allow themselves to let go.

Many women are greatly relieved when they learn that it is perfectly natural to ejaculate and that the fluid is different from urine. The glands that produce the fluid are closely parallel to the male prostate. Both male and female glands derive from the same embryonic tissue, have glands, and ducts. Both structures wrap around the urethra and both produce secretions.

When speaking with women who ejaculate and are fearful of allowing themselves to climax with their partners, I encourage them to practice alone at first, using a vibrator if they are resistant to using their hands. They should put down a big bath towel and allow themselves to complete their orgasm without fear of a partner's response.

When a woman becomes comfortable with her own experience, she should then have a very frank discussion with her partner. Armed with both literature and personal pleasure, she should be confident that her partner would enjoy her newfound ability to fully join in sexual passion.

While not every woman will experience these phenomenon's the fact that certain woman do and that it is perfectly normal should be noted and celebrated.

Multiple Orgasms: Although the term is self-explanatory, it is news to many women that they can have more than one orgasm. These women usually believe this myth because they model after their male partner's responses. She will often engage in intercourse after a brief experience of foreplay and then have intercourse immediately. After her partner ejaculates she feels "it's all over." This practice is often the simple explanation for dry, sore, unfulfilling sex. If a woman realizes that she can have at least two orgasms with oral pleasure, hand stimulation or vibrator assistance before intercourse, she is more likely to lubricate naturally, and have a lot more enjoyment from vaginal penetration, even perhaps "coming together" with her partner simply because she is now truly engaged and highly stimulated. Her clitoris is fully engorged, and she will be more able to position her partner to keep it stimulated.

Anyone interested to learn more about the G Spot, Female Ejaculation or multiple orgasms should read Good Vibrations Guide to The G Spot written by Cathy Winks. It is a very informative little book giving a wonderful explanation of these topics along with lots of other information. Details are in the appendix of this book.

Human beings have devised endless ways to display and demonstrate their sexuality. If we don't grow, we stagnate. Education frees us from old, outdated belief systems that we only hold to be true because no one has told us otherwise.

Pubococcygeus (PC) muscle Kegal Exercises for Women

The PC muscle supports all the pelvic organs; it forms a sling into which the bladder and uterus fall. It is therefore imperative that women keep this muscle toned in order to maintain urine continence and support the uterus throughout life. An easy way to be certain you are using the correct muscle is to sit on the toilet with knees as far apart as possible and start and stop the flow of urine. Do not be upset if you have difficulty stopping the flow - that will take a while. Don't expect results immediately. A regular exercise routine over a period of several months is often necessary before appreciable progress is noted.

All exercises should be done at various intervals throughout the day so the muscles will not become fatigued or tender. If soreness develops, cut down on the number and work up to the prescribed number. If you do the exercises at times you consistently do things, this will act as a reminder, i.e. driving car, sitting at a desk, washing dishes, talking on the phone, changing diapers, etc. Try and do a few exercises before getting up in the morning so all the weight of the internal organs is not on the muscle.

Once good muscle tone is established, maintenance exercises should be continued throughout your life where ten to twenty five contractions and flicks a day should be sufficient.

- Contracting PC muscle and holding for three seconds

- Contracting PC muscle rapidly (flicking)

- Breathing deeply, sucking air in and tightening the PC muscle as air is inhaled

- Bear down as if having a bowel movement or giving birth. As you relax from bearing down, tighten the PC muscle. Especially valuable just prior to intercourse.

Pubococcygeus (PC) Muscle Kegal Exercises for Men

In order to be certain that you are focusing on the correct muscle, you need to know that this muscle enables you to raise your penis. As with the women, it is the muscle which when flexed will stop the flow of urine. Additionally for men, when you have an erection, it is the muscle that, flexed and released, helps you raise and lower your penis. Putting a Kleenex over your erect penis and doing this exercise gives you a visual of your muscle action. The PC muscle supports the genitals for both men and women, and its good muscle tone can help enhance sexual relations. The contractions of this muscle are a major part of orgasm. It can also be utilized to help control orgasmic response. Good muscle tone can mean increased blood circulation and increased sexual awareness and responsiveness.

As with the ladies, practice each exercise while doing routine things such as driving, sitting at a desk, standing in line, doing dishes or changing diapers (omit the visual aide and do the exercise with a flaccid penis). Once good muscle tone is established, maintenance exercises should be continued throughout your life where ten to twenty five contractions and flicks a day should be sufficient.

- Tighten the PC muscle and hold it tightened for a slow count of three. Then relax.

- Tighten and release the PC muscle as fast as possible for a period of ten seconds. This flickering approximates the muscle's behavior during orgasm.

- Breathe in deeply, tightening the PC muscle as you inhale. Then release.

- Bear down as though having a bowel movement. Then relax from bearing down. As you relax these muscles, tighten the PC muscle.

Sensate Focus Exercises

I would like to extend special recognition to my friend Dr. Beverlee Filloy (who sadly passed away in 2007) for sharing her years of experience with me and giving me permission to use these exercises, which she developed from the work of Masters and Johnson, whom she trained with.

These exercises are assigned in a graduated process.

Appointment or date time is to be arranged between partners at a time when interruptions can be avoided. (Children away or asleep, phones or beepers off).

Giver in each exercise setting may enhance the background by using fragrant candles, darkening the room, playing soft music and adding flowers as desired. Be certain these additions are not irritants to receiver and that they will not distract from participants attention to one another.

In the hair caress, each couple decides who will give and who will receive and who will alternate in subsequent exercises. For example, if the male partner is the first giver for the hair exercise, he will be the initial receiver in the foot caress. Within each set of exercises, the couple will reverse roles. At the conclusion of the first set, the couple may decide to continue to the second half (reversing roles) or agree upon a date within a few days to complete the second half.

The purpose of these assignments is to explore positive touch experiences that do not place a demand for further sex-focused contact. If, following the exercise, couples agree that they wish to pleasure each other or themselves further, there is a ban on penile-vaginal intercourse, no ban on intimate touch or orgasm. Each partner has the right and obligation to say NO, if that is the inner feeling. To enhance communication about touch, it is crucial that following the exercise, each person reflect and confides to the partner the positive feelings experienced, e.g. "I felt dreamy" or "Your gentleness was so wonderful." It is important to be authentic and express POSITIVE feelings in one's own words.

To repeat, the basic purpose is to experiment and communicate about touch. Some will find these exercises sexually arousing; others will experience different reactions or a mix of feelings; some may dislike certain ones. Concentrate on the positive parts and be open to both receiving and giving roles. It is a special privilege to touch and be touched.

Remember, these are caresses conveying tenderness, not with the deeper pressure of massage!

Use the blank Love Note pages following each exercise to track your progress.

Hair Caress

Arrange comfortable seating, with giver in chair affording good back support and receiver with pillow under buttocks. Clothing or robe should be loose, non-restricting. Remove eyeglasses, jewelry and watches and loosen sleeves. Have hairbrush and/or combs available to giver (selected by receiver).

Assume position with receivers back to giver's lap. Both partners' eyes and mouths closed as exercise begins. Giver begins to stroke hair (with brush, fingers, comb, as giver wishes). Generally, slow, long gentle motions are preferred. If receiver is uncomfortable, one hand can be placed on giver's hand to demonstrate desired pressure and location or to use a different implement (e.g. discard comb, substitute brush).

Proceed to caress hair, in silence, for at least ten to fifteen minutes. Giver gives "goodbye" pat to hair and then holds partner's head in loving embrace. Couple can then open eyes and greet each other, subsequently share with each other positive aspects of the experience. For example, "Your hair is so soft" or "I felt pampered." It depends on actual feelings, but don't be critical; for example, rather than "You were heavy-handed," comment about liking the light touches.

To complete the course, partners switch roles, repeat preparations seeking comfort and brush selection. This may be done immediately following the first set or postponed to a later agreed upon time within a few days.

Love Notes

Love Notes

Foot Caress

Partners select comfortable chair, position chair against wall and use pillows as necessary so that receiver's head, neck and back are comfortably supported. Giver may also prefer a cushion for seated position. Giver prepares basin (plastic or metal tub) with comfortably warm water and a second container with warm water into which is placed a container of liquid soap and one of baby oil to be warmed. A large bath towel will be needed to place in giver's lap. Both giver and receiver should be comfortably dressed (perhaps robes) and should remove watches, jewelry and eyeglasses.

Invite receiver to sit in previously arranged chair; giver should remove shoes and stockings, roll up pant legs if necessary. Ask receiver to test water temperature with one foot; add warm or cold water as necessary. Place towel over giver's lap. Be certain that giver is at proper distance so receiver's leg can be fully extended.

Place both of receiver's feet into basin, close eyes and mouth (both giver and receiver). Apply warmed liquid soap to one foot (leaving the other in basin) and begin caressing. Move hands slowly and lovingly over all surfaces of foot and each toe, only up to calf). Try different touches, e.g. long strokes, circular motions, whole hands, front and back, use inner wrists. Giver's hands are "making love to a foot." If any tickling occurs, increase pressure initially. Continue caressing, adding soap as necessary to minimize friction. Dry feet gently after caressing both. Wrap one foot in a warm towel while using selected moisturizer to continue gentle massage so that the whole experience lasts for approximately ten minutes at least, longer if desired. Receiver is to be "open" to this gift.

At conclusion giver rewraps both feet and cradles close to chest. Both participants reflect on positive aspects of this experience. Open eyes and greet partner. Leisurely, each expresses positive emotions engendered by this assignment, for example, "relaxing," "sensual," "soothing" are typical responses for both giver and receiver. Also, confide what kinds of touch were most pleasing. Giver replaces stockings and shoes for receiver, if necessary. Roles (giver/receiver) can be switched at this point or a different time set-aside within a few days.

Love Notes

Love Notes

Face Caress

Arrange pillows or pads on floor so that giver's back is supported by wall space and there is ample room for receiver to place head in giver's lap, with body fully extended.

Receiver selects oil or cream to be applied to face; a hair band can be used to protect hair from cream if desired. Watches, jewelry, and eyeglasses should be removed and giver's sleeves rolled up if necessary. Clothing for both should be comfortable. A bath towel for the giver's lap will be needed along with supply of oil or cream within arm's reach.

Assume positions described above, both close eyes and keep mouth shut. Giver applies a small amount of oil or cream on the back of one hand (to warm) and gradually begins to apply to partner's face, beginning with the forehead; using both hands, spread with wing like motions over forehead. After various repetitions, apply oil/cream to chin area, gradually move up sides of face to temple area, and linger before moving on to cheeks, using circular or upward strokes. Gradually move to upper lip area and on to nose and up to brows stroking to outside. Very lightly, with one fingertip, stroke the eyelids and lips, before bringing hands to cup chin. Remain still.

Receiver then places hands over giver's hands and "shows," by receiver moving hands to guide the giver's, to areas of particular pleasure, demonstrating strokes and pressure desired. Receiver removes hands and giver "follows" information just provided by receiver. Receiver's hands may be replaced to give further information.

As giver is concluding the caress (15 to 20 minutes), cup the chin area again; remaining still; each is to reflect on the positives of the experience. When ready, open eyes and greet partner. Offer tissue for receiver to wipe or blot face, as desired.

Following pattern in previous exercises, share positive feeling and experiences with partner. Reversal of roles may take place at this point or may be postponed to a later time.

Love Notes

Love Notes

85

Bathing Caress

Giver draws water in tub to temperature that (s)he believes will suit receiver. Receiver chooses soaps to be used. Some padding or cushion is prepared for giver's knees. Giver removes jewelry, watches, (s)he is comfortably dressed (usually in a robe), no long sleeves. Receiver may be in street clothes or robe, with jewelry removed. Both remove eyeglasses. Do not use bubble bath.

Caress: Giver asks receiver to test water temperature for comfort, then gently disrobes receiver and places clothes appropriately (no bundles on the floor), then helps receiver into tub. Giver kneels at side of tub with soap available, lathers hands and proceeds to lightly caress receiver's entire body with slow loving strokes. (Does not give any greater attention to erotic parts of body. Elbows and knees get equal caressing as breasts or genitals). Does not use soap on genitals.

Both participants should remain largely silent unless real discomfort requires comments and should keep eyes closed as much as possible, this allows both partners to become aware of their deep feelings and responses to being nurtured and taken care of and to taking care of someone with no agenda.

At conclusion, some receivers may wish to shower to remove any soapy residue. While this should be discussed in advance, receiver may make a decision after the bath.

Giver assists receiver from the tub, envelops in large towel, patting or lightly rubbing until receiver is thoroughly dry. (Don't forget between toes).

Following the exercise, each person is to comment on the positive aspects. The reverse (giver-receiver) roles can be postponed to later if discussed.

Love Notes

Love Notes

Body Caress

This caress requires at least one hour's time, two, if both partners are to give and receive. Privacy and leisure time are very significant, preparation is especially important. This is rewarding work!

The best arrangement would be a chaise lounge covered with large towel or sheet placed on a pad on floor in warm, non-drafty area, where temperature at floor level can be warm enough for a naked body. Beds are generally not recommended because of back strain on giver.

The giver makes above arrangements in advance as well as preparing and warming oil or lotion selected by receiver. There are many oils available today and if receiver has a favorite this should be used. However, Kama Sutra oil is highly recommended. If a lotion or cream is selected, be sure it has no alcohol content (which dries and cakes). Bath powder may be substituted if desired, be careful that none is inhaled. It is suggested that in advance, product be tested on inside of receiver's arm.

Warming oil or cream is best accomplished by having a plastic container or ice bucket filled with very warm water (but tolerable for giver's hand). These to be placed within reasonable reach of the giver. Giver should arrange for small pad or cushion on which he or she can sit or kneel. Also handy near-by may be box of tissues and/or bath towel to remove oil, if desired.

Giver, after these preparations, invites receiver to

selected site and gently disrobes receiver, assists partner to lie face down on the pad. Giver, taking massage oil/powder from warm water, applies it to hands, begins caress at upper back, using long flowing strokes from nape of neck out to arms and hands, moving from spine out. Then from spine out over ribs, working down spine to buttocks. Renews lubricant as needed.

Once in area of buttocks, giver glides his/her hands over buttocks, down the outside of legs, with fingers pointed to floor. Caress feet and proceeds up inner thighs, over buttocks, keeping fingers pointed downward in what becomes almost a breaststroke swimming motion. Hands moving from center of body outward.

When all of receiver's back, arms and feet have been caressed, giver gently turns receiver to side position and lies behind him/her (like "spoons"). Tries to match receiver's breathing ("two hearts beating as one"). After four or five minutes, turns receiver so he/ she is lying on back.

Proceeds as before, caressing neck, shoulders, arms, abdomen, over genitals and down outside of legs, fingers pointed to floor. Caresses feet and proceeds up inner thighs, passing over genitals without dwelling in this area. Turns partner to other side and spoons again. Follows receiver's breathing pattern for five minutes.

If giver is female, completes body caress with breast caress. Male is gently turned on his back. Giver anoints her breasts with additional lubricant (e.g. oil) then kneels (using pad or pillow) over partner, supports her body with hands or forearms and moves her breasts over torso to provide additional sensual touch for her partner. They lie together ("spoon" style) for a few minutes, reflecting on positives of overall experience (in role of giver or receiver).

If giver is male, completes the body caress with similar caress, uses genitals (penis and testicles) well lubricated, caresses woman's torso from kneeling position to provide an additional sensual touch for his partner. Replicate lying together, reflecting on positives in both giving and receiving. Share those thoughts with mate.

If sexual arousal takes place, partners may elect to pleasure each other, enjoy self-pleasure, or simply enjoy the presence of such vital feelings but penile-vaginal intercourse is banned following this caress, as in all others. The object is to find pleasure throughout the total body, both in giving and receiving.

Love Notes

Love Notes

Sexual Caress

Follow directions for body caress, but with less time involved, omitting breathing together and breast/genital aspects unless both partners agree to include them and time permits. Do be sure to allow time at end to cuddle and share positive feedback and simply relish the afterglow.

Using oil or cream of receiver's choice, pleasure over abdomen and inner thighs of partner before touching vulva or genitals. If giver is male, he gently touches the labia (outer lips) and follows them toward perianal area (between vulva and anus); then softly touches the inner lips and clitoral area. When the woman signals her readiness, the man inserts his index finger (well lubricated) into the vagina and holds still. A finger cot may be used for a menopausal woman or one having fragile vaginal tissue. The woman attempts to flex her Pubococcygeus muscle so both can be aware of its movement. The man then begins to stroke in and out of the vagina around the PC muscle, beginning at 6:00 o'clock. If the woman is aroused, she may request her partner stimulate her to climax (his choice). She may pleasure herself (vibrators can be fun, for either gender, or she may choose to enjoy simply the feeling of arousal). As a conclusion, the couple may cuddle for a few minutes before sharing feelings and special sensations.

If giver is female, the above procedures are followed. When the woman begins the genital caress, she gently caresses testicles and perianal area before fondling shaft of the penis and coronal ridge and crown of the penis, using ample lubrication.

If an erection occurs, the couple practice squeeze technique in which the man signals his partner that he is close to orgasm, she then applies the squeeze technique where pressure is applied, gently but firmly, to the head of the penis (the coronal ridge), uses thumb and fore-finger for a count of ten to twelve. Erection will subside to some extent; woman continues to pleasure her partner until he again signals the approach of orgasm, she again applies the squeeze. If no erection occurs, postpone squeeze technique practice.

At the end of the allotted time, as noted above, the man may pleasure himself to climax if desired or he may ask his partner to continue pleasuring him; it is her choice to continue. If the man does not feel like having an orgasm at this time, he is free to simply enjoy his arousal and may choose to end the exercise at this point. Be sure to embrace/cuddle before exchanging information about emotions and sensations.

Love Notes

97

Love Notes

Summary

The most important message here is to be open with yourself and your partner. Listen, share your thoughts and try to create a win, win. Negotiate; don't judge! Be open to trying something new. You can live your fantasy. You simply have to believe it and be willing to change (even though change is the hardest thing for us to accept).

Remember, nothing you think or do is original or unique, except in your own perception of the experience. Whatever you want has already been done and written about, so go for it and enjoy!

Healthy Intimacy and Sexuality
for All Ages
Respect Without Judgment

Suggested Reading

Anand, M. & Hussey L. *The Art of Sexual Ecstasy.*
Putnam Publishing Group, 1989

Barbach, I. *For Other: Sharing Sexual Intimacy.*
NAL, 1983

Barbach, I & Geisinger, D. L. *Going The Distance:
Finding and Keeping Lifelong Love.* Nal/Dutton, 1993

Barbach, L., *For Yourself: The Fulfillment of Female
Sexuality.* Doubleday & Company, 2000

Barbach, L., *The Pause: Positive Approaches to Menopause.*
AL/Dolton, 1993 Rev. 2000

Berman, J. & Berman, L. *For Women Only, A
Revolutionary Guide to Reclaiming Your Sex Life.* Owl
Books, Henry Holt & Company, 2005

Cario, Laura. *The Change Before The Change.* Bantam
Books, 2005

Collins, Joseph. *What's Your Menopause Type?* Prima
Health. 1999

Comfort, A. & Rubenstein, J. *The New Joy of Sex: A Gourmet Guide to Lovemaking in the Nineties.* Pocket Books, 1992

Corn L. *101 Nights of GRRReat Sex.* Park Avenue Publishers, 1995

Joannides, Paul. *The Guide to Getting It On.* Goofy Foot Press, 1996

Dodson, B. *Sex for One: the Joy of Self-loving.* Random House, Inc., 1995

Ellison, Carol Rinkleib. *Women's Sexualities, Generations of Women Share Intimate Secrets of Sexual Self-Acceptance.* New Harbinger Publications, 2006

Singer-Kaplan, H. *How to Overcome Premature Ejaculation.* Brunner/Mazel, 1989

Hendrix, H. *Getting the Love You Want: A Guide for Couple.* Harper Trade, 1989

Kline-Graber, G & H. *Woman's Orgasm: A Guide to Sexual Satisfaction.* Bobbs-Merrill, 1975

Lee, John R., Zava, David. Hopkins, Virginia. *What Your Doctor May Not Tell You About Breast Cancer, How Hormone Balance Can Save Your Life.* Warner Books, 2005

Levine, Stephen. *Sexuality in Mid-Life.* Plenum Press, 1998

Love, Patricia, & Robinson, J. *Hot Monogamy Essential Steps to More Passionate, Intimate Love-Making.* CreateSpace Independent Publishing Platform, 2012

Milsten, R & Slowinski, J. *The Sexual Male: Problems and Solutions,* W.W. Norton & Co., 1999

Mordechai-Gottman, J & Silver, N. *The Seven Principles for Making Marriage Work.* Crown Publishing Group, 1999

Mordechai-Gottman, J. & Silver, N. *Why Marriages Succeed or Fail: And How You Can Make Yours Last.* Simon & Schuster, 1999

Mordechai-Gottman, J. & Markman, H. Gonso, J. & Notarius, C. *A Couples Guide to Communication.* Research Press Company, 1980

Muir, C & C. *Tantra: The Art of Conscious Loving.* Mercury House, 1989

Northrup, C. *Women's Bodies, Women's Wisdom: Creating Physical and Emotional Health and Healing.* Bantam, 1998

Northrup, C. *The Wisdom of Menopause: Creating Physical and Emotional Health and Healing During the Change.* Bantam, 2010

Ogden, G. *Women Who Love Sex.* Pocket, 1995

Reiss, Uzzi. *Natural Hormone Balance For Women.* Pocket Books, 2002

Schnarch, D. *Passionate Marriage: Love, Sex and Intimacy in Emotionally Committed Relationships.* Henry Holt & Company, Inc., 1998

Sachs, J. *Sensual Rejuvenation.* Dell Publishing, 2008

Stubbs K. R. PhD. *The Clitoral Kiss: A Guide to Oral Sex.* Secret Garden, 1993

Stubbs K.R. PhD. *Secret Sexual Positions: Ancient Positions for Modern Lovers.* Secret Gardens, 1998

Tannen, D. *You Don't Understand: Women and Men in Conversation.* Random House Inc., 1991

Walz, T. & Blum, N. *Sexual Health in Later Life.* Lexington Books, 1987

Weed, S. *Menopausal Years: The Wise Woman Way, Alternative Approaches for Women 30-90.* Ash Tree Publishing, 2002

Winks, Cathy. *The G Spot. The Good Vibrations Guide.* Down There Press, 1998

Zilbergeld, B. & Ullman, J. *Male Sexuality: A Guide to Sexual Fulfillment.* Little Brown & Co., 1978

Zilbergeld, B. *The New Male Sexuality.* Random House, 1999

Helpful Books on Illness and Sexual Function

Berman, Jennifer MD. & Laura PhD. *For Women Only: A Revolutionary Guide to Overcoming Sexual Dysfunction & Reclaiming Your Sex Life.*
Henry Holt & Co.,Inc., 2005

Dackman, L. *Up Front: Sex and the Post-Mastectomy Woman.* Viking Penguin, 1990

Goldstein, I. & Rothstein, L. *The Potent Male: Fact, Fiction, Future.* Putnam Publishing Group, 1990

Schover, L.R. *Sexuality and Fertility After Cancer.* Wiley, John & Sons, Inc., 1997

Schover, L.R. & Jensen, S.B. *Sexuality and Chronic Illness: A Comprehensive Approach.* Guildford Press, 1988

Shover, L.R. *Sexuality and Cancer for Women.* The American Cancer Society, 1988

Shover, L.R. *Sexuality and Cancer for Men.* The American Cancer Society, 1988

Sipski, M.L. *Sexual Function in People With Disability and Chronic Illness: A Health Profession's Guide.* Aspen Publications, 1997

Websites

www.improveintimacy.com
The Author, Dr. Fran Fisher's website

www.HIVUnsite.ucsf.edu
For patients, practitioners and researchers (HIVI AIDS information)

www.aasect.org
American Association of Sexuality Educators, Counselors and Therapists.

www.ashastd.org
American Social Health Association

www.askisador.com - Sexuality Forum

www.ATSA.com
Association for the Treatment of Sexual Abusers

www.bodymindandintimacy.com

www.condomania.com

www.gayhealth.com

www.gurl.com
Website for teenage girls. Get advice about life, love, relationships, sex, our body and how to deal with girl issues.

www.sinclairinstitute.com - The Sinclair Institute is a source of sexual health products for adults who want to improve the quality of intimacy and sex in their relationship.

www.kaiserreproductive.com - Kaiser's site for information on reproductive health

www.nerve.com - A beautiful site celebrating the human body through yoga.

www.sexandrelationships.org

Publications Resources Supporting Prevention Activities & Survivor Healing

www.sexed.org
Site of Marty Klein, sex educator and speaker.

www.sexhelp.com
Addiction treatment and counseling

www.Sexualhealth.com
Online clinic

www.sexuality.org
General Resources on Sexuality

www.sexualtherapy.com
National sex therapist's directory and resources

www.sexetc.com
Sex education for Teens by Teens.

www.sexhelp.com
Sex addition and recovery

Education

www.sexualhealth.com - Great for Women

www.sexuality.org - General resources on sexuality

www.sexualtherapy.com   - National Sex Therapist's Directory

www.sexscience.org - Study of Sexuality

www.sexualityresources.com - A Woman's Touch Sexuality Resource Center

www.Siecus.org - Education and information about sexuality and sexual and reproductive health.

Sexuality Video and Erotica Resources

www.candidaroyalle.com
Candida Royale Videos – Femme Productions Institute

www.goodvibes.com
Good Vibrations

www.adameve.com
Adam & Eve

www.Xandria.com
Xandria Collection

www.sinclairinstitute.com
Sinclair Institute
Educational sexuality videos, Ordinary
Couples/Extraordinary Sex Volumes 1-2

About the Author

Dr. Fran Fisher

After a twenty-five year commitment to her previous careers of homemaker, mother and registered nurse across a variety of health care specialties, Dr. Fisher made a remarkable discovery in her middle years. She had never discussed the effect of any medical disease or condition on the intimate sexual life of her patients. Seeking to remedy this omission, she embarked on a course of study, which led to her becoming a Clinical Educational Sexologist with a Ph.D. in Human Sexuality.

Because of past experience and a gift for public speaking, she now occupies a unique position in the field of sexuality education. A seasoned speaker and presenter on TV and radio, she developed workshops and seminars for various specialized rehabilitation facilities and helped sensitize the medical profession to the sexual needs of their patients. Using a thorough knowledge of her subject, she guarantees results to those willing to listen, learn, and change.

To quote Dr. David Satcher, "It is necessary to appreciate what sexual health is, that it is connected with both physical and mental health, and that it is important throughout the entire lifespan, not just the reproductive years ... that the many aspects of sexuality include not only the physical, but the mental and spiritual as well. Sexuality is fundamental to human life. While the problems usually associated with sexual behavior are real and need to be addressed, human sexuality also has significant meaning and value in each individual's life." Firmly believing this message, Dr. Fisher works tirelessly to educate with Humor, Respect and without Judgment.

To contact Dr. Fisher for booking information or consultations to discuss your issues in comfort and privacy:
916-791-8426
drfran@improveintimacy.com

What others are saying about Dr. Fran Fisher:

"Dr. Fisher is an outstanding educator in the field of Human Sexuality. She is honest, forthright and passionate about the importance of sexuality in human relationships, and she has the ability to help her clients and students address these topics comfortably."

Dr. Barnaby B. Barratt,
Former Professor of Family Medicine, Psychology and Behavioral Neuroscience, Wayne State University School of Medicine, Michigan. Former President of the American Association of Sex Educators, Counselors, and Therapists.

"Thank you for your entertaining and illuminating talk on sexuality for patients with cardiovascular disease. As in the past you evidenced an excellent ability to bridge the often-sensitive gap between fact and mythology regarding sexuality and people with medical illness. The patients, psychology staff and I very much appreciated your sensitivity to the patients and their questions. Your warmth and wit created an environment conducive for patients to explore this sometimes-uncomfortable yet vitally important area of functioning. Your use of examples, reference materials and samples of devices patients may use was greatly appreciated by all. We will surely welcome your return for another series of lectures to our patients and wish you well in your work."

Doug Cort, PhD
Director - Psychology Section
UCDMC Preventive Cardiology Program

What Members of the Community are Saying

"I really enjoyed the presentation. I think the segment on knowing your own body is vital. So many women are too embarrassed or shy to explore themselves and then wonder why they cannot have orgasms. Most importantly, we as women, need to get comfortable talking not only to our partners but to other women about our sexual needs." *– Katie (21 years old)*

"I appreciate the demonstration of various tools/toys. All the handouts are wonderful. I applaud your open and intelligent presentation." *- Louisa*

"Very useful, the first time I can talk to someone else than to my husband." *- Phyllis*

"I thoroughly enjoyed the class. I really appreciated all of the information and presented in such a fun way! Thank you - you did a wonderful, fun, educational and very professional presentation." *- Susan.*